T5-CQD-436

*Jeff Munroe*

# SIGNS AND WONDERS IN THE GOSPEL OF JOHN

# six unsolved mysteries

**CRC PUBLICATIONS**
Grand Rapids, Michigan

Prime-Time Bible Studies series. Six
Unsolved Mysteries: Signs and Wonders in
the Gospel of John, © 1997, CRC
Publications, 2850 Kalamazoo Ave. SE,
Grand Rapids, MI 49560. All rights
reserved. With the exception of brief
excerpts for review purposes, no part of
this book may be reproduced in any
manner whatsoever without written
permission from the publishers.

Printed in the U.S.A. on recycled paper. ❀
1-800-333-8300

ISBN 1-56212-266-5

10 9 8 7 6 5 4 3 2 1

# ONTENTS

Introduction ................................................................................................................5

1   Can't You Read the Signs? (John 2:1-11)................................................................9

2   More than Bread (John 6:1-15, 25-37) ................................................................17

3   Sight for the Blind (John 9) ................................................................................23

4   Lord, He Stinketh (John 11) ................................................................................31

5   Resurrecting the Resurrection (John 20) ..............................................................39

6   The First and Last Words (John 21) ....................................................................47

Evaluation Form ........................................................................................................57

# ▲ NTRODUCTION

## Prime-Time Bible Studies

*Six Unsolved Mysteries* is part of the *Prime-Time Bible Studies* series. Each course in the series offers six sessions of Bible study aimed primarily at high school juniors and seniors; the series is also appropriate for recent high school graduates.

The textbook is the Bible itself, usually studied on a chapter-by-chapter basis and carefully exegeted in the Reformed/Presbyterian tradition. Teaching and learning methods are varied and appealing, encouraging group members to work cooperatively or individually to discover for themselves the richness of the biblical material.

*Prime-Time Bible Studies* include a helpful leader's guide and a book of perforated handouts for each group member.

## Six Unsolved Mysteries

### Theme

Why did Jesus work miracles? What do his miracles say to us? What signs and wonders does God work in our lives today? These are among the questions we'll consider as we look at six "unsolved mysteries" in the gospel of John.

We begin with the changing of water into wine, which John describes as "the first of [Christ's] miraculous signs." Then we follow Jesus as he stretches a lunch for one little boy into a meal for thousands, gives a man born blind a brand-new look at life, calls a dead man out of a tomb, breaks out of his own tomb on Easter morning, and arranges a record catch for some tired fishermen. Following John's emphasis, we'll look beyond each miracle to see what it tells us about the One who worked the miracle, so that we "may believe that Jesus is the Christ, the Son of God, and . . . by believing . . . have life in his name" (John 20:31).

This course will also challenge us to become more aware of the amazing work of God in our own lives. Answers to prayers, unexpected moments of grace, the friendship of others, the beauty and power of creation . . . such are the "signs and wonders" that point us toward God.

## Goals

This six-session course on signs and wonders in the gospel of John has four general goals:

- ■ to describe the nature, purpose, and impact of six miracles Jesus performed as recorded in the gospel of John
- ■ to explain what these miracles show us about Jesus
- ■ to make us more aware of the amazing work of God in our lives
- ■ to help us respond in faith and with committed lives

## Materials

To lead this course you'll need this leader's guide (explained below) and one book of handouts for yourself and each group member. Prior to each meeting time, tear the necessary handouts from each book and have them ready to distribute at the appropriate points in the session. A list of other materials is included with each session.

## Audience and General Approach

This course contains six group-study sessions. It is intended for use by high school students and young adults in church school, youth group, or retreat settings.

Ideally, you should have a full hour for each of the six sessions. You'll find there are plenty of activities to fill sixty minutes or more. Should you have less time, you'll need to trim or omit some suggested steps.

This course uses many group activities of the sort that youth consistently rank above "leader presentation" as effective teaching/learning methods. These activities are lively and fun, and they help people learn from each other. They're designed to encourage participants to examine Scripture, to apply sound Bible study principles, and to draw their own conclusions.

This course does not require homework, a feature that today's busy young people will appreciate. Instead, suggestions are given (via a follow-up handout for each session) for daily devotions, journal-keeping, and other readings or activities that promote spiritual growth (a top-rated goal of high schoolers, according to a recent survey taken by CRC Publications).

## Leader's Role

As leader, you'll want to get to know each group member, to keep the various activities moving and on track, to facilitate discussion and interaction, and to model what it means to be open to God's Word and Spirit. Try to cultivate an atmosphere of openness with the group that allows participants to feel free and secure.

You needn't be an expert theologian or Bible scholar. Studying the Bible passage during the week and reading the Perspective section for each session will help you lead with competence and confidence. Remember that "I don't know" is an acceptable answer that will build your credibility better than bluffing your way through. Promise to find out what you don't know (or ask an interested group member to do so). Your pastor is a good resource for pursuing puzzling questions.

## Using the Leader's Guide

This leader's guide will help you prepare for and lead the sessions. It will tell you when and how to use the handouts that accompany this course.

Each session plan has three parts: *Purpose, Perspective,* and *Procedure.*

The Purpose section spells out the goals of each session. Knowing your goals will help you keep the session on track and avoid distractions.

The Perspective section provides you with important theological and biblical background information. It's intended to enrich your own insights so that you can supply the group with informed input and direction (but please resist lecturing on its contents).

Between the Perspective and Procedure sections you'll find a list of materials you will need to lead each session. Each group member will need a pen and a Bible (we suggest the NIV; you may also want to keep an *NIV Study Bible* handy for reference). Keep a newsprint pad and markers handy. Consider providing snacks to help get each session off to a relaxed start (you may want to ask group members to take turns bringing a treat).

The Materials section also lists the Handouts you'll need for each session. Handouts are numbered sequentially throughout the course. From time to time you may want to omit a handout or substitute an activity of your own in its place.

The Procedure section furnishes step-by-step directions (with time estimates totaling forty-five to sixty minutes) to help you reach the goals of the session. These steps suggest a variety of approaches that blend individual, small group, and whole group activities. You as the leader know your group and their needs. So you'll want to make those adjustments that help meet the needs of your group and achieve the goals of the session. Don't let the structure prevent you from responding to personal concerns.

Options are listed at the end of each session plan. They provide alternatives to the regular steps of the session. If you feel that a given activity is not suitable for your group, you may find that one of the options will work better.

## Planning a Bible Study Core

*Prime-Time Bible Studies* courses offer a varied menu for your high schoolers. But they also can be used to form a solid Bible study core for one or more years. To do that, start with the Old Testament foundation course *Stones, Thrones, and a Valley of Bones.* Follow this with one or more Old Testament Bible studies (see list on back cover). Then use the New Testament foundation course *Gospels, Acts, and End-Time Tracts.* Follow that with one or more New Testament Bible studies (see list on back cover). For variety or to extend the curriculum still further, add some four-session

*LifeWise* courses between the Bible studies. Check the CRC Publications catalog or call us (1-800-333-8300) for *LifeWise* titles or more information on the *Prime-Time* courses.

## Evaluation Forms

At the end of this leader's guide is a short evaluation form for you (the leader) to fill out. An evaluation form for group members is included in the handouts for this course. You can help us improve the *Prime-Time Bible Studies* series by using these forms to share your reactions about this course.

Please send completed evaluations to

CRC Publications
Prime-Time Bible Studies
2850 Kalamazoo Ave. SE
Grand Rapids, MI 49560

Thank you.

# CAN'T YOU READ THE SIGNS?

## Scripture

John 2:1-11

## Purpose

> *Sign, sign, everywhere a sign . . . Do this, don't do that, can't you read the signs?*

These words from a rock-and-roll golden oldie could serve as a miniature introduction to the gospel of John. Those who can read the signs see Jesus, the Messiah, the Word become flesh. John 2:11 says, "This, the first of his miraculous signs, Jesus performed in Cana of Galilee. He thus revealed his glory, and his disciples put their faith in him." In other words, when Jesus turned water into wine, the disciples read the sign and recognized that Jesus was God in human form.

This session has four goals:

- to describe Jesus' first miracle
- to see the significance of miracles as signs in John's gospel
- to identify some of the signs we see in our own lives that point us to who Jesus really is
- to describe what practical difference it makes when we really see who Jesus is

## Perspective

The gospel of John is different from those of Matthew, Mark, and Luke. The other three are often called the synoptic gospels. "Synoptic" literally means "see together"; Matthew, Mark, and Luke tend to see the events of Jesus' life in the same way. John, in contrast to the synoptics, follows a different chronological order and records events, such as the miracle at Cana, that are not found in the other three.

Other more subtle variations are worth noting. For instance, Matthew, Mark, and Luke usually emphasize the miraculous event itself and the power that's displayed. John tends to emphasize the significance of the miracle and what it tells us about Jesus, rather than the miracle itself.

The turning of water into wine illustrates this. If we are looking for a mighty act of God, this miracle, on the surface, seems a bit trivial. In the midst of a world so overwhelmed by darkness, despair, disease, and death, the Savior of the world launches his ministry by turning water into wine so some people can have a nice wedding party. And he does it in Cana of Galilee, which is a bit like saying that he performs his first miracle in Podunk Corners. Although Podunk Corners probably is a wonderful place to live, doing miracles there does not guarantee the press coverage and fame one would receive in New York, London, or Jerusalem.

But here is John, painstakingly filling in all the details: he describes the time and place of the miracle, the number of water jars on hand, what the jars were used for, even the amount of water each jar held. With a little quick calculating we can estimate that Jesus turned approximately one-hundred-and-fifty gallons of water into wine.

Why such detail? Because John is writing about real people and real events, and in the midst of these real people and events God is present. The Word has become flesh (John 1:14). Something very important is happening here. True, John portrays miracles as signs, yet they are not separated from the day-to-day events of life. God does not operate only on mountaintops or in some unseen spiritual realm. There is no separation of the spiritual world from the physical world; rather, God acts in extraordinary ways in the ordinary events of life.

Of course this story is also ripe with meaning and significance. As in every miracle in John's gospel, all kinds of signs and symbols are at work here. The wine is wine, but it is not just wine.

A challenge of teaching this story to young people may be getting them to unload some of our current cultural baggage about wine and see it instead through the eyes of those who were present with Jesus at the wedding in Cana. The Bible does warn about becoming drunk on wine (Eph. 5:18), but we need to remember that drinking wine was almost as natural to these people as drinking water or milk or Coke is to us today. One reason for its popularity was the scarcity of good, potable water.

Unlike our culture, in which it is customary for the bride's family to host the wedding reception, in Jesus' day the party would have been at the groom's home. And it wouldn't have been unusual for the wedding feast to have lasted up to seven days. The host would have served his best wine first, while the guests' senses were sharpest, saving the second-rate stuff for later in the celebration.

On a symbolic level, "they have no more wine" is as much a statement about the nature of Israel's disobedience as it is a statement about this party. Isaiah 5:1-7 says that Israel was a vineyard planted by God, but that it yielded only bad grapes. Thus, the marriage at Cana symbolizes the marriage of God and his people—they have no wine, and the wedding that should have been joyful threatens to turn into an embarrassing disaster. All of the ritual water in the world cannot restore the relationship between God and his people. Only Jesus can and will.

The six stone water jars stand as symbols of the Old Covenant. They are there for the rites of purification required by Jewish law. What Jesus does by turning the purification water into wine is symbolic of the New Covenant. In the Old Covenant, water was used again and again to symbolically wash away the sins of the people; in the New Covenant, the sacrifice of Jesus will wash away the sins of the people once and for all.

Throughout the gospel of John, Jesus replaces the feasts and ceremonies of the Old Covenant. Something new is happening. This miracle in Cana is the first example, and it produces belief in the disciples, who see the sign for what it is and appreciate its meaning. Earlier, the disciples believed Jesus was the Messiah (1:41), and he promised them they would see great things (1:50). But the other guests at the party don't see God at all; they are surprised only because the best wine comes at the end of the party.(And they get another pretty good surprise, because the best wine is drawn from the jars they had washed in earlier!)

One other note about this passage: Jesus' exchange with Mary sounds disrespectful to modern ears. Actually, this is a good example of how meaning is sometimes lost in translation. "Woman" was a term of respect, but one that put Mary at a distance, like our "madam." Note that Mary was encouraged, rather than discouraged, by Jesus' response to her.

In summary, what Jesus revealed about himself in this first sign is that he actually is the Messiah whom God has sent to take away the sins of the people and restore them to real fellowship with God. Although, as he told his mother, his "hour" of crucifixion had not yet come, Jesus already offered a glimpse of what he had come to do. By changing water to wine, Jesus revealed that he would wash away our sins and bring us to real celebration. He had come to make us enjoy forever our new relationship with God. While the guests partied on, Jesus' disciples caught the hint. They saw it and put their faith in him.

## Materials

1. Handouts 1 and 2
2. Pens or pencils
3. Bibles
4. Blocks or Legos, needles/thread
5. Props for talk show: name labels for characters, microphone or tin can, table
6. 3" x 5" notecards
7. Theme notebooks for journals (optional)

## Procedure

■  **Step 1**
   **Losing Depth (10 minutes)**

If this is the first meeting of your group, have a quick round of informal introductions. If you've brought snacks, now might be a good time to sample them. Do what you can to establish a relaxed, informal, accepting atmosphere.

To introduce your topic for the next six sessions, ask group members to try several simple exercises that call for some manual dexterity. They should do the exercises with one eye closed.

Explain that when we close one eye, we not only lose a fair amount of our peripheral vision but also a great deal of our depth perception. The world flattens, and we have a hard time accurately judging distances. *(Author's note:* I experienced this firsthand when, wearing an eye patch after eye surgery, I stabbed the table attempting to get mayonnaise from a jar.)

Here are some suggested exercises (add some of your own based on your experiments at home):

■ Hold a pen or pencil at arm's length. Use the other hand to place another pen or pencil directly on top of the first one.
■ Make a tower of blocks or Legos, again working an arm's length away. Take turns placing a block on the tower.
■ Thread a needle while holding it at arm's length.
■ Extend an arm directly in front of your nose. Bring your index finger slowly to your nose (not difficult until you get close!).
■ Extend your arms wide apart. Bring your left middle finger and your right middle finger together in front of you.

After trying a couple of these exercises, explain that they're just a way of helping us remember how to look at the miracles in the gospel of John, our topic for the next six sessions. We can look at these miracles flatly, as if we are looking with only one eye— but that way we'll miss a lot. Or we can look at them with both eyes wide open and see them in more depth. It's a matter of perception.

Point out that the first mystery or miracle is found in John 2:1-11, the wedding at Cana. Before reading this passage, have the group members find John 20:30-31 in their Bibles. Ask someone to read it aloud. Explain briefly that John calls Jesus' miracles "signs" that reveal the nature of Jesus.

Ask for a volunteer to read John 2:1-11 to the group members as they follow along in their Bibles.

■   **Step 2**
    **Who Saw What? (20-30 minutes)**
To get at some of the differences in perception about the miracle at Cana, present a short talk show. Distribute Handout 1 ("Talk Show") and read the opening paragraph, the directions for the host, the guests, and the audience. Ask for volunteers to play the host, the bridegroom, the banquet master, Mary, and Nathanael. The rest of the group can be the studio audience.

Give everyone a few minutes to prepare, then arrange the guests in front of the audience. Have name tags available for the guests. Give the host a mike (or a tin can) and seat him or her behind a desk or table, if possible. Feel free to add other props just for fun. Encourage the kids to really get into the talk-show mode.

After the talk show is presented, ask what conclusions the group can make about the events in Cana. Which characters see this event "flatly" and which see it more in depth? Talk together about the even deeper levels to this story:

■ "They have no more wine" is symbolic of Israel's relationship with God (see Isaiah 5:1-7).
■ The ceremonial washing jugs are symbolic of the Old Covenant.
■ The best wine coming later is symbolic of the New Covenant.

See the Perspective section for additional comments.

■ **Step 3**
  **A Modern Miracle (10-15 minutes)**
Distribute Handout 2 ("God at Work") and ask someone to read it aloud. Then spend a few minutes discussing the questions at the end of the handout.

■ **In your life or the life of someone you know, have unusual events or coincidences happened that could be signs of God's working?**

Be ready with your own example—or one you've heard—to relate to the group. For instance, perhaps you or someone you know was cured of a disease in a way that the doctors can't explain. Or maybe God used a coincidental meeting with an old friend to steer you to a new job.

The monthly magazine *Guideposts* includes a column called "His Mysterious Ways" that will give you additional examples to cite. Check your local library for copies.

■ **What other, perhaps more ordinary, signs do you see that God is for real?**

Talk with your group about such things as unexpected "moments of grace" in our lives, times when we feel God's presence and love through another person's encouraging words or loving acts. Other Christians can show us the face of Christ by even the smallest acts of kindness and caring.

Many of us are especially aware of God's power and love when we receive an answer for something we've long prayed for. And when we say "Thank you, God, for answering my prayer!" God seems very close and very real.

God's creation also points us to God. A quiet walk in the woods, a rainbow after a storm, a crisp fall day—all can point us toward the Creator.

Give your group enough time to think of and share specific examples of their own.

■ One word that may summarize the miracle at Cana is "transformation." Jesus transforms the ordinary washing water into wonderful wine. He also can transform our lives from ordinary into extraordinary. What actual differences can you see that faith in Jesus makes in your life?

This obviously calls for a rather personal response, almost a "testimonial" of sorts. Take time to talk about this with your group. Admit that talking about our own faith— even among friends—isn't easy for most of us. Maybe we worry about sounding like super-Christians who have all the answers or like spiritual wimps who are struggling with all kinds of doubts. There are things we may not be ready to talk about with others. Still, it's very important for our spiritual growth that we learn to share our faith. Doing so among Christian friends is an important first step.

Be ready with your candid response to the question of what actual difference faith in Jesus makes in *your* life. Don't be afraid to admit to struggles and doubts. Set an honest and open tone for group members to imitate. Then ask for volunteers to share their thoughts.

■ **Step 4**
   **Closing (10-15 minutes)**

Distribute one notecard to each person and ask everyone to complete this statement:

■ To me, this miracle shows that Jesus . . .

Ask for volunteers to read their statements aloud.

We suggest you end each of the six sessions in this course with a similar exercise. You may want to collect the cards and return them to group members at the end of the course, when the cards can be used to review the main ideas from the course.

Distribute Handout 3 ("Follow-up") and skim it with the group. It's an optional piece that interested group members can use to carry the insights of today's session into the week ahead.

For those who are motivated to write, each follow-up handout will include a journal proposal. Keeping a journal may sound like a pretty dumb idea to your group—it involves taking time to write at home, and, admittedly, writing isn't exactly on the top ten list of most teens. But growing spiritually is a goal of many teens, and keeping a personal journal is one of the best ways to grow spiritually. You might mention this to your group when you talk to them about the journal proposal in every follow-up handout. And do let the group know that you'll be keeping a journal yourself (refer to things you've written in your journal from time to time during these sessions). You might want to provide inexpensive theme notebooks in which group members can keep their journals for the course.

Each follow-up also includes a "For Your Devotions" section that takes group members back into the passage you studied together. An additional activity or reading is also suggested.

Conclude today's session by sharing this line from Psalm 50:3: "Our God comes and will not be silent." Give the group members a moment of silence in which to think about how they have seen God at work in their lives. Close with sentence prayers of thanks for the signs of God we see in our lives.

## Options

These options offer alternate learning activities that you may want to substitute for some of the regular steps in the session plan.

### 1. Alternate Opening

Rather than using the exercises suggested in Step 1, begin by mentioning the title of this course (*Six Unsolved Mysteries*), then asking each person to mention one or two unsolved mysteries that he or she wonders about. Examples can range from the silly (why mothers always insist on oatmeal for breakfast) to the sublime (what will heaven be like?). Get things started by giving a couple of examples of your own, maybe one serious and one silly.

### 2. Alternate to Talk Show

Read John 2:1-11 as "reader's theater." You'll need readers for Jesus, Mary, the master of the banquet, and a narrator who reads all parts not in quotation marks.

After the reading, ask the group members to take the role of reporters at a news conference. They may ask questions of each character in the story (a raised hand indicates they have a question). The questions should try to get at what each character saw and what it meant to him or her. Follow-up questions are encouraged.

Either you (the leader) or the narrator can act as the moderator of the news conference, directing questions from the reporters to the characters and (optionally) summarizing the conference at the end.

### 3. Sign Journal

Keep a "sign journal" in your meeting place. Each week during this course ask group members to jot down "signs" that they've seen of God at work in their lives or in the lives of people they know. If group members are keeping a journal of their own at home (see Handout 3), they can draw from it to contribute to the "sign journal" of the group.

*Session*

# 2  MORE THAN BREAD

## Scripture

John 6:1-15, 25-37

## Purpose

The same themes that were introduced in John 2 are repeated in John 6. Jesus performs another sign, this time transforming five barley loaves and two dried fish into a feast for thousands. Like the wine in chapter 2, the bread in chapter 6 is a potent symbol. And, as at Cana, the crowd enjoys the benefit of the sign but misses its meaning.

As we have seen, John's purpose in writing is so that we might believe and have life (20:31). This life comes from the spiritual food that Jesus offers, but the crowd that follows him after this miracle only wants bread for their stomachs. Jesus knows they need bread for their souls.

This session has three goals:

- to describe the feeding of the five thousand
- to explain what this sign tells us about Jesus
- to give examples of how we may want the benefits of Christianity without accepting their Giver

## Perspective

The Reformed liturgy for the celebration of the Lord's Supper describes it as a feast of remembrance, communion, and hope, with a threefold significance in the past, present, and future. The same past, present, and future aspects are at work in the sign of Jesus feeding the five thousand in John 6.

John points out that it was close to the time of the Passover, the celebration of God's deliverance of Israel out of Egypt. During the Exodus, God had provided manna or bread from heaven. This great past event was quickly recalled by the Jews present with Jesus when he produced bread on the shores of the Sea of Galilee.

Jesus performs a mighty act, taking the lunch of one boy and transforming it into a meal for thousands. As at Cana, Jesus takes care of the present by satisfying immediate physical needs. Interestingly, the One who can make endless supplies of food gives careful instructions about gathering the leftovers—God provides abundantly but not wastefully.

**17**

This miracle also points forward to the not-so-distant Passover meal when Jesus will again take bread, give thanks (the Greek word used in verse 11 is *eucharist*, meaning "to give thanks"), and distribute it. Jesus makes his understanding of bread as a sign for his body startlingly clear later in this chapter (vv. 50-60)—so startlingly clear, in fact, that these verses (which are beyond the scope of today's lesson) are among the most shocking Jesus ever said and ought to be recalled every time we seek to domesticate him as gentle, meek, and mild.

The crowd that has been fed is swept with the desire to make Jesus their king, but he recognizes that their enthusiasm is not belief. They have followed him into the Galilean wilderness because of his skills as a healer, and now they see that he will feed them as well. Moses had called down bread from heaven and had promised a prophet like himself (Deut. 18:15); perhaps the long-awaited prophet has arrived.

Moses had led them out of slavery in Egypt, and some in the crowd no doubt think that Jesus will lead an uprising against the oppression of Rome. To give in to the crowd's passion would frustrate the purpose of Jesus' mission. He will not be front man for a people's liberation movement, for his is a spiritual kingdom, not an earthly one. Jesus slips away from both the crowd and the disciples, night falls, and those who want to make Jesus king are left, quite literally, in the dark.

This is all exposed a day later when the crowd finds Jesus in Capernaum. He tells them they are looking for him only because of the bread they ate, not because they saw a sign. The bread's delicious, but the bread isn't the point because they'll be hungry again. The people should come to Jesus for bread for their souls, not their stomachs. If they focus only on the bread, they'll be condemned to the perpetual human problem—being on an endless quest for satisfactions that never endure.

Like the woman at the well (John 4) who naively asks for living water so she won't have to keep coming back to the well when she's thirsty, the crowd wants some of this eternal bread so they will never get hungry again. In an agrarian society, this represented a fantastic possibility. They wondered what they'd have to do to get some of this bread. What was the work God required?

The work is belief, Jesus says; a work indeed, but God's work, not ours. Belief is not our accomplishment but God's gift, and the crowd's clamoring for a sign is further proof that they do not believe. A day before they had been miraculously fed; now they demand a sign. They quote Psalm 78:24, and say, in effect, show us a sign like Moses, give us bread from heaven like Moses did, and we'll believe in you like we believed in Moses. Like the old saying about the misuse of statistics, they used Psalm 78 like a drunk uses a lamppost—for support, not illumination.

Jesus answers by exploring the true meaning of Psalm 78: it wasn't Moses who gave the bread, it was God. And it isn't just bread that God gives; above all God gives life. That's what the bread is a sign of. Like people standing in a river hoping it will rain so they can get some water, the Jews ask for a sign while they are looking at it. They ask

Jesus to give them what they want, but they have not learned that Jesus is what they need.

## Materials

1. Handouts 4-5
2. Pens or pencils
3. Bibles
4. Newsprint and markers
5. Various kinds of bread, butter, knives, jam, drinks
6. Notecards, one per person
7. Sign journal (optional—see end of last week's session)

## Procedure

■ **Step 1**
**Bread Basics (10 minutes)**

If you've decided to make a "sign journal" available (see option 3 of last week's session), display it prominently as group members arrive. Invite them to take a moment to record something in the journal. If you've also encouraged them to begin journaling at home (see Handout 3), make some friendly inquiries about how things are going.

Because today's session focuses on bread, a fun way to begin is with a bread-tasting party. Visit a bakery or bagel shop and gather as many different kinds of bread as your budget permits (if you have a kosher store in your area, get some unleavened bread too). Provide jam, butter, knives, plates, and drinks—and enjoy.

While the kids are snacking, ask the group what miracle of Jesus the bread suggests we're going to study today (feeding of the five thousand; if the group is unfamiliar with the Bible, simply tell them this). Then talk about the different meanings of the word *bread:*

■ a delicious bakery product
■ money
■ the things we need to live, as in "our daily bread"
■ how one makes a living, as in "my bread-and-butter"
■ a meal, as in "breaking bread"
■ being aware—as in "knowing which side one's bread is buttered on"
■ the body of Christ
■ manna in the wilderness

Comment that the bread in this miracle in the gospel of John is like the wine at the wedding feast in Cana—on one hand it literally is bread, and on the other hand it is a symbol of much more. In this incident, similar to the wedding story in chapter 2, the crowd focuses only on the bread and misses the deeper meaning of the sign.

■ **Step 2**
**Two Kinds of Bread (20-25 minutes)**

Introduce today's story with comments like these:

> Jesus and his disciples had been through a lot of stress and were heading to an unpopulated area to get away for a break. Jesus' life had been threatened in Jerusalem, and the crush of people in Galilee was so great they "did not even have a chance to eat" (Mark 6:30). While most Jews would have been making a pilgrimage to Jerusalem for the Passover, Jesus wished to avoid more confrontation there and had apparently decided to take the disciples away for a time of quiet rest and spiritual retreat. Because of his healing miracles, though, the crowds swarmed to him even in a remote area.

Distribute Bibles and read John 6:1-15, 25-37. If your group enjoys the "reader's theater" format, ask for volunteers to read the lines of the following characters in today's story:

■ Jesus
■ Philip
■ Andrew
■ the people (can be read in unison by several persons)

Have a narrator read all the lines not in quotation marks.

Distribute Handout 4 ("Two Kinds of Bread") and give group members five minutes or so to work through the ten multiple-choice questions on their own. Then go through the questions together, sampling several responses for every question. Give kids time to explain their answers when necessary. Draw on the Perspective section to help guide your discussion.

The last question, "What would your reaction have been?" leads naturally into the next step of the session.

■ **Step 3**
**What's in It for Me? (10 minutes)**

We often think it would be easy to believe if we had the opportunity to see the things that people who lived at the time of Christ saw. John's gospel makes it very clear that this is simply not true. Plenty who saw did not believe.

The crowd at this miracle enjoyed the bread but didn't understand it. As we've said, the bread's delicious, but the bread isn't the point. Wonder aloud with your group: *Are there current examples of "benefits" of Christianity that we sometimes focus on without really accepting Christ?*

Take a piece of newsprint and label it "What's in It for Me?" Generate a list of the benefits of attending church and being a Christian. Some examples (use a couple to prime the pump, as necessary):

- A Christian lifestyle is healthier; it keeps you out of trouble.
- Church is a good place to meet people who share my values.
- It's easier to make friends with other Christians.
- People trust Christians more.
- Christianity offers sound moral principles on which to build my life.
- Christians feel better about themselves, have greater self-esteem.
- Christians are better equipped to handle life's troubles, problems.
- Christians have hope for the future.
- Christians go to heaven, not to hell.

Talk about how "believing" just for these benefits is different from the kind of belief Jesus described in today's passage. None of the things on this list are bad or evil. But there is an essential ingredient missing: faith. The essence of faith is *relational*. Have someone read John 17:3 aloud: "Now this is eternal life: that they may know you, the only true God, and Jesus Christ, whom you have sent." The path of following Christ moves us away from self-gratification to a life of service, away from a sinful, me-first attitude that leads to death to a self-sacrificing attitude that leads to life.

Michael Casey writes, "The Bible is an instrument of salvation because it challenges our habits, attitudes, and behavior. As soon as it begins to confirm and reinforce our own views it is reduced to the status of a hand puppet or an idol. It no longer brings us closer to God; it simply parrots our own opinions."

One of the great temptations in the Christian life is to subtly reshape God in our image instead of letting God reshape us in his image. Too often we deal with God on our terms instead of submitting to God in obedience on his terms.

- ## Step 4
  ### Closing (5 minutes)

Explain that Jesus' insistence on an intimate, indwelling relationship—graphically expressed through his demand that we eat his flesh and drink his blood—is a turning point in the gospel of John. Have someone read John 6:60, 66-69. Peter's statement is really a confession of faith. Ask your group members to take a moment to consider what their confession is—when confusion reigns about them, what do they think about Jesus?

Distribute notecards and ask everyone to complete this statement:

- This miracle shows me that Jesus . . .

Encourage group members to include their own personal reaction to Jesus in their statements. Be clear that this is not an attempt to manipulate them into a confession they're not ready to make. Their statements should honestly reflect where they are on their spiritual journeys, even if right now they're dealing with doubt or uncertainty. Ask for volunteers to share their statements, and be ready to share your own statement as well.

Distribute Handout 5 ("Follow-up") with its journal proposal and suggested devotions for the week ahead.

Make sure all the bread from step 1 is eaten or going home with someone who will use it (to do so is in keeping with the spirit of this miracle we studied today).

## Options

### 1. Alternate Opening

If the bread-tasting activity won't work out for you, try this instead. Write the word "bread" on your board or on newsprint, and ask group members to write everything that this word brings to mind. They should write as rapidly as they can, without pausing to think or evaluate. Give them two minutes to complete their list. Then go around the circle, letting each person add three items from his or her list without repeating what another person said. Talk about the various meanings that "bread" can have (see step 1).

### 2. Drama

If the group already know the story of the feeding of the five thousand, suggest that they act it out. Assign characters, then block out the major scenes in the story. Give them time to read over what their characters said and did in the actual Bible story from John 6:1-15, 25-37. You may want to supply a few props as well (baskets to hold the food, perhaps some paper fish, some of the bread you brought).

When the actors are ready, proceed with the dramatization. Include the bread tasting described in step 1 as part of the dramatization if you wish.

### 3. Write an Ad

Rather than just make a list of the benefits of being a Christian (see step 3), have group members work in small groups to create advertisements that highlight one such benefit. The advertisements could be for a magazine (supply drawing paper, markers) or for television (kids can give a "testimonial" or act out the benefit they're describing).

### 4. Alternate Closing

For a quiet, meditative kind of ending, play a recording of "Eat This Bread," available from CRC Publications on "In the Presence of Your People."

You could also read Isaiah 53 responsively. The opening section "Who has believed our message?" is especially appropriate for today's session.

# 3 SIGHT FOR THE BLIND

## Scripture

John 9

## Purpose

> In him was life, and that life was the light of men. The light shines in the darkness, but the darkness has not understood it.
>
> John 1:4-5

> "I am the light of the world. Whoever follows me will never walk in darkness, but will have the light of life."
>
> John 8:12

Sight for the blind is a promised sign of the Messiah's arrival (Isa. 29:18; 35:5; 42:7). Like the synoptic gospels, John tells a story of Jesus healing a blind man. True to form, the emphasis in John is not so much on the miracle itself but on what it reveals. The dialogue that follows the miracle indicates that this is not just a random healing of one unfortunate person. The blind man is representative of all humanity. We learn that the world is not divided into those who have sight and those who are blind; rather, it is divided into those who are blind and know it, and those who are blind and think that they can see.

This session has five goals:

■ to describe this miracle and its impact
■ to explain how the Pharisees showed their blindness
■ to give examples of God's work in others
■ to pray for the vision/faith to see God behind the events of our lives
■ to believe and confess God's name

## Perspective

This wonderfully-told story begins with the basic question asked in the face of all human suffering: Why? Why was this man born blind? Whose fault is it?

Addressing this question, Jesus comments on the purpose of the man's blindness rather than its cause. Instead of offering some kind of deep philosophical answer to the problem of human suffering, he offers help and healing. Which would we prefer when faced with life's darkest moments?

Putting mud on the eyes of the blind man, Jesus, the one sent by God, sends the man to wash in a pool called Sent. In following these instructions, the blind man takes his first steps of faith. The light of Christ overcomes the darkness of his eyes, and that light begins to shine through him, as it should shine through every believer who is washed and sent by Jesus.

The man is so utterly changed that his neighbors have trouble recognizing him—he may be the same person but he is a new man (2 Cor. 5:17). He is also unable to give a satisfactory explanation for all that has happened to him—all he knows is that "the man they call Jesus" was behind it. Confounded by his story, his neighbors take him to the "powers that be," the Pharisees. The problem with this is that when the radically new comes, the "powers that be" usually are the most threatened and the last to understand it. The Pharisees are learned in the law, but "the law is only a shadow of the good things that are coming" (Heb. 10:1). You don't put new wine into old wineskins, and you don't ask darkness to explain the light.

The Pharisees are confused and divided because Jesus broke the Sabbath *and* performed a mighty act. They ask the man what he thought of Jesus, and this time he answers, "He is a prophet." The man is moving forward in his understanding of Jesus while the Pharisees are moving backward.

The Pharisees then decide to interrogate the man's parents, hoping to find out that the whole story is a hoax. The parents admit their son was blind and now can see, but are too intimidated to say any more. As one commentator puts it, "The parents fear the authorities, and the authorities fear for their authority."

Calling the man back a second time, the Pharisees put him under oath. This time the man says Jesus is "from God." Three times the blind man humbly confesses his ignorance (vv. 12, 25, and 36), and three times the Pharisees boldly declare what they know (vv. 16, 24, and 29). The lines are clearly drawn as the Pharisees' claims of knowledge pale in comparison to the man's sole claim: "I was blind but now I see." He has no desire to review the details of what he had already plainly told them. Realizing the cracks are beginning to show in the Pharisees' facade, he sarcastically wonders what makes them so curious? Perhaps they would also like to become Jesus' disciples?

Never known for their ability to take an insult, the Pharisees go on the offensive, expelling the man, and noting that, because he was born blind (which they had earlier sought to deny), he must have been "steeped in sin at birth" and is unfit to lecture them. The words of John 1:5 are shown to be true: "The light shines in the darkness, but the darkness has not understood it."

After the Pharisees drive the man out, Jesus finds him, for in contrast to the Pharisees, "whoever comes to me I will never drive away" (6:37). The man's understanding becomes complete as Jesus explains who he is. The one who has seen precious little in his lifetime is told that he has already seen the Son of Man, and he makes his confession and worships.

Jesus makes the meaning of this miracle very clear: the blind who know they are blind are not sinners, but the blind who insist they see are. As Leon Morris paraphrases the man's statement to the Pharisees in verse 30: "This is the really marvelous thing—your unbelief in the face of the evidence is more a miracle than my cure."

As John says, "Light has come into the world, but men loved darkness instead of light because their deeds were evil. Everyone who does evil hates the light and will not come into the light for fear that his deeds will be exposed. But whoever lives by the truth comes into the light, so that it may be seen plainly that what he has done has been done through God" (3:19-21).

It is tempting for us to roll our eyes at the hardheaded Pharisees. But just as John uses the blind man as a representative of all humanity, so also he uses the Pharisees. We too can become blinded by our certainty of what we know about God. We can become judgmental about the faith experiences of others, particularly if they take a form different from ours. We sometimes try to limit God to our own experiences. We do not and cannot control God, yet we find it exceedingly difficult to let him control us. The light we need is not our possession but is offered as a gift, and the appropriate response to that gift is humble worship.

## Materials

1. Handouts 6-8
2. Pens or pencils
3. Bibles
4. Blindfolds
5. Notecards, one per person
6. Sign journal (optional—see end of session 1)

## Procedure

■ **Step 1**
  **Blindfold Walk (10 minutes)**

If you are using a "sign journal," be sure to have it available when group members enter the room today. Encourage them to look at the journal even if they have nothing to contribute to it today.

Begin today's session by giving everyone an opportunity to imagine what it's like to live without sight. Divide into pairs and have one member of each pair put on a blindfold. The blindfolded person's partner then leads the blindfolded person on a silent walk for three minutes. Their only communication should be by hand. The walk can be in the halls of your church or other meeting area, or, weather permitting, outside. It should be a little challenging, with some obstacles to get around. The partners should reverse roles after three minutes.

After the exercise, ask what it was like and what other senses they used when they were blindfolded. You may wish to point out that, in today's story, Jesus heals by involving senses other than sight when he spits, makes mud, puts it onto the blind man's eyes, and then sends him to wash.

*Note:* This session assumes that all the kids in your group are physically sighted. If this is not the case, adjust the session plan so that any persons who are sight-impaired will not feel uncomfortable. Sensitively draw on the experiences of such persons to help the rest of the group better understand what it's like to live with limited or no eyesight.

■ **Step 2**
**Who's Really Blind? (20-25 minutes)**

Distribute Handout 6 ("Who's Really Blind?") and ask for volunteers to read the parts that are listed on the handout. Double up on some roles if you have fewer than eleven people in your group. This interesting story from John 9 unfolds like a drama and can be fun to act out as well as read (no need to use real mud, though!).

Give your characters time to underline the places where they come in. They can also decide what tone of voice to use when reading their lines (neighbors: curious, skeptical; Pharisees: puzzled, hostile; parents: cautious, worried; Bart: sincere, at times annoyed, almost sarcastic; Jesus: compassionate to Bart, harsh to Pharisees).

Present the drama, then use the questions at the end to discuss it. Have Bibles ready for the group to use.

**1. Jesus knew that the Pharisees would consider his healing this blind man as breaking the Sabbath. Why do you think he did things that he knew would bother them?**

Jesus did not agree with the Pharisee's interpretation of what the Sabbath meant. He wouldn't be bound by their legalistic understandings—when he saw a person in need, he responded to that person's need, regardless of what day of the week it was, for "the Son of Man is Lord of the Sabbath" (Luke 6:5). As we saw in the story of water turned into wine, one of the things Jesus does is bring a new understanding to the laws of the Old Covenant: "the Sabbath was made for man, not man for the Sabbath" (Mark 2:27).

Jesus also did not seem very concerned about offending the Pharisees and other religious leaders. There is a tension here—sometimes we idealize Jesus as the "Prince of Peace" and fail to remember that at times he could be very confrontational. Eventually he got under the skin of the authorities so much that they decided to kill him.

**2. Why are some of the man's neighbors and the Pharisees so unwilling to accept this miracle?**

Have someone read verses 8-12 from chapter 9. Some of the doubt of the neighbors may be due to the healed man's changed person (see 2 Cor. 5:17). Besides, he doesn't do very well at answering their questions. So they tend to doubt the walking, talking evidence that is before them, and they bring their doubt to the religious leaders who are supposed to know how to deal with such things.

To summarize the reactions of the Pharisees, have someone read verses 16-19, 24, 28-29, 34. As the Perspective section points out, the Pharisees are too entrenched in their learning and traditions to be open to something so radically new. They feel threatened. And, besides, Jesus is a Sabbath-breaker, a sinner. So they end up closing their eyes to the miracle and to the one who worked it.

**3. Use your Bible to trace how the healed man grows in his understanding of who Jesus is.**

Note these changes in the healed man's thinking about Jesus:

■ Verse 11: Jesus is "the man they call Jesus."
■ Verse 17: Jesus is "a prophet."
■ Verse 27: Jesus is someone who has disciples; in fact, the healed man counts himself as one of them.
■ Verse 32: Jesus is "from God."
■ Verse 38: Jesus is the "Lord," in whom the healed man confesses his belief and whom he worships.

**4. How do the events in this story illustrate what Jesus says at the end, that "for judgment I have come into this world, so that the blind will see and those who see will become blind"?**

This statement helps make John's main point clear: that the world is in darkness, and Jesus is the light of the world. Some are drawn to the light, and others are repelled by the light. John had already said this in 3:19-21; he also develops this theme in 12:37-50. See the Perspective section for additional comments.

**5. In what ways are we sometimes like the blind man who was healed?**

Like the blind man, we too are in the dark without Jesus. We need to be healed of our sinfulness. Whenever we humbly grope toward the light in this dark world, whenever we finally confess that Jesus is Lord, whenever we truly worship him, we are like the blind man. Thank God that Jesus is the Light that overcomes the darkness!

**6. In what ways are we sometimes like the Pharisees?**

We are like the Pharisees when—

■ we scoff at others' faith experiences.
■ we are certain we have God figured out.
■ we see Christianity as a set of rules instead of a dynamic relationship.
■ all we can do is look back on past faith experiences instead of point to current ones.

■ **Step 3**
  **Helping Each Other See (10-15 minutes)**

Distribute Handout 7 ("Helping Each Other See") and read it aloud to the group. Be sure to allow time for questions and comments.

Then give every group member a chance to be the focus of the group's attention. When the group focuses on a person, other group members tell that person how they see God acting in them. As leader, you will want to think ahead about the members of your group and be ready to say something positive about every person.

Make sure the group focuses on you too—it's healthy for them to have a chance to affirm you. After everyone has had a turn, ask the group to sit quietly for a couple of minutes and reflect on what has just been said to them.

*Note:* Some groups will be somewhat uncomfortable with this exercise at first. If you sense that it's asking too much of your group and just isn't working, have them put their comments on notecards and give them to the group member being affirmed. This, of course, restricts the impact to just the member being affirmed. But it's better than dropping the exercise altogether.

■ **Step 4**
  **Closing (5 minutes)**

Distribute notecards and ask each person to complete the usual statement: "This miracle shows me that Jesus. . . ."

Close today's session by inviting each group member to pray silently for the vision and faith to see God more clearly in their lives. Encourage them to think of any special circumstances in their lives in which they wish they could see God more clearly.

Distribute Handout 8 ("Follow-up") and encourage group members to use it at home this week.

## Options

### 1. Alternate Openings

Instead of the blindfold walk, try one of these exercises:

■ Invite a person who is sight-impaired to speak to your group about what his or her life is like. After a brief presentation, give group members a chance to ask questions. Ask your presenter to give suggestions about how sighted persons can best relate to and possibly assist persons who are sight-impaired.
■ Talk together about some of the entries in your "sign journal."
■ Listen to or look at the words of some hymns that have references to blindness ("Amazing Grace," "Blindman," "Open Our Eyes, Lord," etc.). Talk together about why this theme is so prevalent in all types of Christian music.

■ Have each person list three traits they think are typical of "spiritual blindness." Make a master list on newsprint and, later in the session, see how many of the terms apply to the Pharisees (and possibly to ourselves!).

## 2. Alternate to Drama and Discussion

John 9 is, among other things, a well-told story. In your preparation, read it through several times, savoring its irony, its humor, and its insights into the human heart. Think about how the characters sounded as they delivered their lines. Practice reading it aloud a few times, until you feel you have it down well.

Share some of your thoughts about this story with your group, then ask them to follow along in their Bibles as you read it to them.

Afterwards, use questions like these for discussion:

■ Do you like this story? If so, what do you like about it?
■ What would you want to say to the Pharisees in this story? To the blind man? To Jesus?
■ Where do you see yourself in the story?

## 3. Alternate to "Seeing God in Others" and Closing

Ask each person to jot down a few thoughts on his or her spiritual vision. Where does it seem reasonably clear and strong? Where are some blind spots? Or, if 10 represents perfect spiritual vision and 1 represents spiritual blindness, where on the scale would he or she fall? Allow time for thinking and jotting some notes. Then pair off, sharing as much of what was written as is comfortable and helpful. Conclude with the partners praying for each other, either aloud or silently.

# 4 LORD, HE STINKETH

## Scripture

John 11

## Purpose

The raising of Lazarus is the last and greatest of the signs John records before the all-inclusive sign of Jesus' resurrection. As we have seen, John's purpose in recording these signs is so that we may believe and have life in his name (20:31). This sign, the closest to that purpose, serves as a fitting climax to Jesus' earthly ministry and results directly in his death. As Raymond Brown writes in his commentary on John, "Here we have another instance of the pedagogical genius of the Fourth Gospel . . . All Jesus' miracles are signs of what he is and what he has come to give man, but in none of them does the sign more closely approach the reality than in the gift of life . . . the suggestion that the supreme miracle of giving life to man leads to the death of Jesus offers a dramatic paradox worthy of summing up Jesus' career."

There is an abundance of material in this chapter, but we will focus mainly on three comments made to and about Jesus. The first is made by both Martha and Mary: "Lord, if you had been here my brother would not have died" (vv. 21, 32). Second is Martha's great confession in verse 27, "I believe you are the Christ, the Son of God." Third is the high priest Caiaphas's unintentionally prophetic statement in verse 50: "It is better for you that one man die for the people than that the whole nation perish."

This session has four goals:

■ to explain the purpose of this miracle
■ to give examples of our own search for God in the face of suffering and death
■ to tell how knowing that Jesus is the resurrection and the life affects our view of suffering and death
■ to make Martha's confession our own

## Perspective

The old English of the King James Version of the Bible gives a humorous twist to a tragic time. Lazarus has been in the tomb four days when Jesus arrives and gives the command to roll back the stone.

"Lord, he stinketh," says Martha.

He stinketh indeed. After four days there was no doubt that Lazarus was really dead and had begun the smelly process of decomposing. Martha and Mary, who believed in Jesus, had hoped he could do something to save their brother. But he hadn't come when they needed him, and now it was too late. So they ask, in effect, "Jesus, where were you when we needed you the most?"

It is not an unprecedented question. In his anguish Job says

> If only I knew where to find him;
> if only I could go to his dwelling!
> I would state my case before him
> and fill my mouth with arguments.
> I would find out what he would answer me,
> and consider what he would say. . . .
> But if I go to the east, he is not there;
> if I go to the west, I do not find him.
> When he is at work in the north, I do not see him;
> when he turns to the south, I catch no glimpse of him.

—Job 23:3-5, 8-9

Frederick Buechner says that what Job was really after was "not an explanation of suffering but the revelation that even in the midst of suffering there is a God who is with us and for us and will never let us go."

In this way, the raising of Lazarus is reminiscent of the healing of the man born blind. Jesus offers no explanations; instead, he takes action. Death, in all its finality, does not have the final word. Jesus has the final word, and his word is life. "Your brother will rise again," he tells Martha, and she hears this like family members at an infinite number of funerals who have been told that their loved ones have gone to a better place. She believes in the doctrine of the resurrection, but she does not really feel it, for her loss is great. No, Jesus tells her, you don't understand. The doctrine of the resurrection is alive; it has a face and a name. Because faith is relational, it is dramatic, not frozen in definition, but changing, and in some ways unpredictable. "I am the resurrection and the life." Death is not a wall but a door, a door to a life that is not bounded by death.

There are two possible responses to this. One is confession, like Martha's: "You are the Christ, the Son of God" (11:27). These words mirror John 20:31, and the promised result is delivered with the command "Lazarus, come out." Of course one day Lazarus will die again, but from this day on, life is revealed as a greater power than death.

The other response is unbelief in the face of the evidence. This leads to death: "If we let him go on like this, everyone will believe in him, and then the Romans will come and take away both our place and our nation. . . . So from that day on they plotted to take his life" (11:48, 53).

The religious leaders do not deny the fact that Jesus is doing miraculous signs, but their political fears overwhelm any spiritual interest they may have. In their arrogance, they worry about "our place" and "our nation," failing to acknowledge that the temple and people belong to God, not to them. Caiaphas, the high priest, the one who yearly would enter the holy place to make atonement for the people, offers a solution. The death of one man is a small price to pay for the preservation of everything they hold dear.

We, of course, hear his words in a completely different way than he meant them. One man *will* die for all the people, and one man's blood *will* atone for the sins of the people in a way that the sacrificial blood offered annually by the high priest never could. God is using the schemes of the Sanhedrin to work his divine purpose. What they mean for harm, God will use for good.

Chapter 11 ends with the Passover being at hand, and while the Jews prepare themselves and gossip about Jesus, they are unaware that the greatest sacrifice ever is about to be offered, a sacrifice that will put an end to the sacrificial system forever. The next chapter begins with Mary anointing Jesus' body and is followed by his triumphal entry into Jerusalem. It will be a memorable Passover.

Jesus wept because of the suffering of Lazarus, the grief of Mary and Martha, and perhaps even the presence of darkness, disease, and death in God's world. He doesn't minimize or trivialize the reality and pain of human experience. But in word and deed he proclaims that, as far as life is concerned, not even death is the end of the story. This is the core of our faith, "for God so loved the world that he gave his one and only Son, that whoever believes in him shall not perish but have eternal life" (John 3:16).

## Materials

1. Handouts 9-11
2. Pens or pencils
3. Bibles
4. Obituaries from the daily newspaper
5. Newsprint with questions (see step 2)
6. Notecards
7. Sign journal (optional)

## PROCEDURE

■ **Step 1**
**Telling Our Stories (15 minutes)**

As group members arrive, invite them to read or write in the "sign journal."

Begin today's session by unfolding a recent newspaper and casually paging through it, maybe reading a headline here and there. Ask what parts of the paper, if any, your group members tend to read first. Then mention the obituary column. Does anyone *ever* read it? Take a minute to read a couple of obituaries to the group (if possible, choose one of an older person, one of a younger person).

Talk about how we as a culture tend to deny the existence of death. It's a subject that immediately makes us uncomfortable—we'd rather not think about it. That's why most of us—even people as ancient as thirty or forty—seldom look at the obituaries. It's only when we get really old, when our friends start dying off, that we might make a habit of reading the obituaries.

But death is persistent, and in spite of our desires it reaches every one of us. Someday each of us in the group will be the subject of an obituary.

Distribute Handout 9 ("Is It Dead?") and choose two group members to read the dialogue from *My Name Is Asher Lev* by Chaim Potok. The other group members can follow along.

After the reading, ask the group if they have ever had a "close call" or if someone close to them has died. If the group is too large to give everyone a chance to speak, divide into small groups so everyone has a chance to tell his or her story. Encourage people to share what they felt when they were going through this experience. What questions did the experience raise for them? How did it affect their relationship with God? Did those who had a near-death experience change in any way as a result of the experience? Do they know anyone else who has changed as a result of a near-death experience?

*Note:* If any of your group members have recently lost someone they love, you will need to think carefully about how to handle today's session. An exercise such as the above could be much too painful for someone still in the grieving process. Consider calling such a person prior to today's session so that he or she can decide whether or not to attend. If the person does attend, choose your session activities carefully and be supportive and sensitive.

■ **Step 2**
**Digging Deeper (15 minutes)**

Explain that today's passage from John deals with death as directly as any passage in the Bible. Distribute Bibles and have group members read John 11 in turns.

Have the following questions written on a sheet of newsprint. Divide into pairs and assign each pair to one or more of the questions. With larger groups, assign the same question to different pairs. With smaller groups, assign more than one question to each pair. After five minutes, have the pairs report their answers.

**1. Both Martha and Mary say the same thing to Jesus in verses 21 and 32. Try restating their words as a question we might ask of God. When in our lives might we ask such a question?**

The question of the two sisters sounds something like this: "Why didn't you come when we asked you to?" or "Where were you when we needed you?" We tend to ask

**34**

the same question when we're faced with suffering, trials, and troubles in our lives. It's then that we most need God's presence. Point out any connections that exist between this and the group's own stories that were shared earlier.

**2. Whose confession of faith in this chapter echoes John 20:31 (a key verse in John)? When in our lives might Jesus ask us, "Do you believe this?"**

John 20:31 promises that belief in Jesus gives life. Martha echoes this in verse 27: "I believe that you are the Christ, the Son of God." At times of crisis, of disappointment, of grief, of suffering, of the death of loved ones, our beliefs are tested. It's easy to say "Jesus is the Christ, the Son of God, and he's in control of my life" when all is going well. But when the chips are down, these words do not come quite so easily to most of us. To her credit, Martha makes a wonderful confession at a time when she was assailed by grief and puzzled by Jesus' delayed response. Despite her confession, however, she doesn't comprehend what Jesus is going to do for Lazarus. God surprises us as our lives with him unfold.

**3. Caiaphas, the high priest, makes an unintentionally prophetic statement in verse 50. How did he mean it? How does John understand it? What does this tell us about God?**

Caiaphas meant that killing Jesus would save the Sanhedrin by letting them remain in Rome's favor. John understands that the death of Jesus would save all humanity. The plans of Caiaphas reveal God's sovereign power. He can take the most evil schemes and use them for good. This also is a pillar of our faith—that even when life seems darkest, God is present and active.

**4. What does this chapter show you about Jesus? Mention at least three things.**

Some possible responses are:

■ Jesus has absolute power over death. He is the resurrection and the life.
■ Jesus cares deeply about human sorrow. Twice John says Jesus was "deeply moved." And the shortest verse in the Bible says even more: "Jesus wept."
■ Jesus worked miracles for a definite reason: "that they may believe that you [God] sent me."
■ Jesus is able to use the bleakest moments in our lives to strengthen our faith.

■ **Step 3**
**New Realities (10-15 minutes)**

The resurrection is the center of our faith. It changes our comprehension of reality. That's the point to get across in this part of the session.

Have the pairs from the previous step join one other pair. Then distribute Handout 10 ("Resurrection Realities") to each person. Ask the small groups to read the handout and to fill in the columns, listing how the resurrection affects our understanding of a number of things.

Give the groups up to ten minutes to finish. If time permits, quickly sample a response in each category. If time is running out, the discussion can be limited to the small groups.

Sample answers:

|  | No Resurrection | Resurrection |
| --- | --- | --- |
| Death | The end of life | Gateway to next part of life |
| Life | Not as powerful as death | More powerful than death |
| Suffering | Diminishes life; avoid at all cost | May teach many lessons; Jesus redeemed us through it |
| Christ | A great teacher but just a man | The Son of God |
| Salvation | No salvation; live for this life alone | Eternal life; this life is just a taste of our future glory |
| Stress | A necessary part of an uncertain future | Peace/contentment in knowing what's ahead |
| Money | Most important thing in life; get all you can. | A useful tool with no lasting value; "Hearses don't have luggage racks" |
| Grades | Key to your future | Important but not ultimate |
| Future Job | Another key to future | Another way of serving God |

■ **Step 4**
**Closing (5-10 minutes)**

If you're using the notecard question at the end of each session ("This miracle shows me that Jesus . . . "), repeat that procedure today.

Maya Angelou's wonderful poem "Just Like Job" expresses both the anguish of someone searching for God and the hopefulness of someone who lives confident in the promises of God. This kind of hopefulness can be traced to the resurrection. Distribute Handout 11 ("Follow-up") and use the poem as your closing prayer (have group members take turns reading the verses or read it yourself).

Encourage group members to use the poem at home this week as part of their devotions.

## Options

### 1. Alternate Opening

Rather than reading the selection from Potok, have group members write their own obituary. What would they like to be remembered for? Allow enough time for writing (use notecards) and for sharing.

### 2. Alternate Bible Study

If you want a ready-made set of questions to use (rather than the questions on newsprint), use the "For Your Devotions" section of Handout 11 ("Follow-up"). Here you'll find John 11 divided into four sections, each with its own set of questions.

You can assign the questions to four small groups or have individuals be responsible for different questions.

### 3. Alternate Step 3

If your group is imaginative and would enjoy responding in a nonverbal way, try this exercise instead of Handout 10. Give each group several sheets of newsprint and some markers, crayons, or chalk. Tell them their task is simple: to make a poster that illustrates what the resurrection means to them and/or how it affects their lives. What, to them, visually represents the new life the resurrection of Christ brings to each of us?

The idea here is not fancy artwork but creative expression of the central truth of our faith. For example, a poster might show a green vine forcing its way up through an asphalt parking lot. Or it could show a sun shedding light on different aspects of our lives—school, home, church, sports, leisure, and so on. Captions can be added to the posters.

Set a definite time limit, then ask each group to explain its work.

### 4. Guest

Have a visitor from Hospice come and talk about his or her work with people who are dying.

*Session*

# 5 RESURRECTING THE RESURRECTION

## Scripture

John 20

## Purpose

Chapter 20 of John shows once again how John's accounts of events often take a different slant than the accounts of the other gospel writers. In the synoptic gospels, the resurrection of Christ is a happening of such cosmic proportions that it causes cataclysmic occurrences like earthquakes and the appearance of angels who look like lightning and strike fear into the hearts of everyone they encounter. But John's picture is more subtle. Details—such as John running faster than Peter—are included because that is the way it happened. But the focus in John is on the meaning of the resurrection.

This meaning is seen primarily in restored personal relationships. Mary, Peter, Thomas, John, and the other disciples all have their relationships with Jesus restored. The resurrection of Jesus Christ makes it possible for us, also, to have a personal relationship with him. This is a relationship that death cannot destroy.

This session has four goals:

- to describe the various reactions to the resurrection reported in John 20, and to say with which character's reaction we identify
- to explain the point of this great miracle
- to realize that (like the disciples) we don't need to have things all sorted out or be perfect Christians to believe
- to respond to the challenge of verse 31

## Perspective

"Mary."

With one word the world is changed.

"Mary."

The good shepherd knows his sheep and calls them by name.

"Mary."

Racked with grief, groping in the dark for the stolen body of her Lord, Mary encounters the risen Christ. With one word he resurrects Mary, turning her "mourning into dancing," to use Walter Wangerin's phrase. "Mary," Jesus says, "go to my brothers (*brothers!* Not *go tell those fools who deserted me* but *brothers*) and tell them 'I am returning to my Father and your Father, to my God and your God.'"

With these inclusive words, things become startlingly different because "to all who received him, to those who believed in his name, he gave the right to become children of God" (1:12).

This is a new relationship—no longer master and pupil, but brothers and sisters, kin.

Imagine Mary's feelings on that incredible day. She started the day in grief, a grief that was compounded by the agony of the missing body. Then she sees a man and thinks, "Who else but the gardener would be here so early?" So she asks the gardener if he had taken the body (at least she got that right—for that man has indeed moved the body!). Of course it is the Lord—we all see it coming, but Mary somehow doesn't. He is alive! Finally, she crashes into the room and tells the skeptical disciples, "I have seen the Lord!" It was a day of wild and wide mood swings for Mary.

What must Peter have felt? Or John? Alerted by Mary, they race to find a not-quite-empty tomb. If the body had been stolen, the grave clothes would also be gone, for what thief would take the time to unravel the grave clothes and then carry around a naked corpse? This is a puzzle for Peter, but John believes the grave clothes have been left behind by the risen Christ.

The evidence of the grave clothes and Mary's testimony are apparently not enough to convince the whole group, because that night they huddle in fear behind locked doors. Suddenly Christ is in their midst, showing the marks of his crucifixion, and the two dominant emotions of the disciples—fear and sorrow—are changed into joy. Emotions are not the only thing to change, though. The disciples must change too. The fearful band must be transformed by the Holy Spirit. Forty times John has described Jesus as the one sent by the Father; now the disciples are to be sent in the same manner. In the words of John Stott, here the Great Commission is stated in an incarnational form: "As the Father has sent me, I am sending you."

Thomas, of course, misses this appearance and earns a spot in history as the role model for future generations of doubters, skeptics, and cynics. Jesus reappears a week later and shows his wounds to Thomas, making him the last of the eyewitnesses to the resurrection mentioned by John. For Thomas, seeing is believing, but future believers will have no such tangible sign. They will be blessed because they believe without seeing. This is where we are, and it can be a difficult place to be. Frederick Buechner writes, "Even though he said the greater blessing is for those who can believe without seeing, it's hard to imagine that there's a believer anywhere who wouldn't have traded places with Thomas, given the chance, and seen that face and heard that voice and touched those ruined hands."

During this session, you will be wondering with your group where we are in this resurrection scene. Are we like Mary, joyfully proclaiming that Jesus is alive but first needing to hear him call our names? Are we like Peter, confused by his own mixed feelings, not really knowing what to think, but finally believing and living up to his calling? Or are we with the doubters and Thomas, needing a sign before we can say, "My Lord and my God"?

Thankfully for all of us, Jesus doesn't require perfect faith. Instead, he simply calls our names and we come to him, just as we are, warts and all. That's the great message to get across to your kids today.

"Mary, Dirk, Josh, Keri . . . "

When Jesus calls our names, our world changes.

## Materials

1. Handouts 12-13
2. Pens or pencils
3. Bibles
4. Notecards
5. Newsprint/markers
6. *The Book of God* by Walter Wangerin, Jr.—either on video or audiotape (optional)
7. Sign journal (optional)

## Procedure

■ **Step 1**
**A Fresh Look at the Resurrection (10 minutes)**

If you're using the sign journal option, don't forget to invite kids to look it over or add to it at the beginning of the session. You may want to take a minute or two to mention some of the things that group members have written in the journal.

Today's session will focus on the resurrection. Chances are that you and the kids in your group have heard this story so often that the power and drama of the event have been nudged aside by the tiresome monotony of repetition. Or perhaps some of your group aren't all that familiar with this key story of Scripture. In either case, a fresh, dramatic look at the Easter story will help make it even more amazing and memorable.

In *The Book of God* Walter Wangerin, Jr., retells the story of the resurrection (and other biblical stories) with detail and flair, much as a modern novelist might do. This is not a new paraphrase or interpretation, nor is it restricted to the gospel of John. It is a good storyteller skillfully weaving the threads of the resurrection accounts together. You may want to use one of the following options to bring Wangerin into your group in a personal way.

1. *The Book of God* is available in a video format with Wangerin telling some personal stories and reading excerpts from the book. His words are punctuated with songs by Ken Medema. The video is about an hour long, and the resurrection story is at the end of the tape.

2. *The Book of God* is also available on cassette tape, with Wangerin reading the entire 850-page text. The resurrection account is on the final tape.

The video, cassette set, and book are all available from Zondervan Publishing. Check your local bookstore. Or you can borrow the video from TRAVARCA, the lending library of the RCA and CRC (1-800-968-7221).

Should neither of these options work for you, use the excerpt on Handout 12. You'll want to practice reading the story a couple of times before today's session.

We suggest you distribute Handout 12 ("A Fresh Look at the Resurrection"), give some background explanation similar to the above, then read it to the group. Afterward, ask for reactions. Did the story format help make the resurrection account more vivid and real?

## ■ Step 2
### Character Sketches (20 minutes)

After the reading, distribute Bibles and ask everyone to turn to John 20. Explain that in the first part of the chapter John focuses on Mary Magdalene's visit to the tomb. Point out that this does not contradict the other gospels or the account we just heard, in which several women visit the tomb. Even in John's gospel Mary says, "*we* don't know where they have put him" (20:2).

Point out that John tells what happened next, after Mary blurts out her astonishing news to the disciples. Take turns reading John 20:19-31 aloud.

Next, divide into three groups. Ask group 1 to focus on the character of Mary Magdalene, group 2 on Peter, group 3 on Thomas (if necessary to keep group size down to three or four, assign more than one group to a character).

Tell each group their task is the same: to tell about or show the change that their character experienced in today's story. They may show this change in any of the following ways:

- ■ by using newsprint to write "before" and "after" words and/or to make sketches showing the change
- ■ by pantomiming the change
- ■ by acting out the change
- ■ by creating "freeze frames" showing their character before and after the change
- ■ by using any other approach they can dream up that portrays the change in an interesting way

They should draw on the information from the story on Handout 12, from John 20, and from what they may already know about these characters. In addition, they should look up these passages (jot them on your board or newsprint):

- Group 1 (Mary Magdalene): Luke 8:1-3
- Group 2 (Peter): Matthew 16:16-18; John 18:15-18, 25-27
- Group 3 (Thomas): John 11:16; 14:5-7

Allow about ten minutes for preparation. Then ask the groups to give their presentations. Following are a few notes that you as leader may use to help summarize the group's report.

**Mary Magdalene:** We can only imagine Mary's life before Jesus drove seven demons out of her (Luke 8:2). After that, though, she proved to be a loving and devoted follower of her Lord. We see her faithfulness by her early morning visit to the tomb, where she and the other women who cared for Jesus in life now care for his body in death. At the tomb she breaks down and weeps. So profound is her grief that she fails to recognize her risen Lord. But when she does, her sadness turns to wild joy and she races to the disciples to shout the incredible good news.

**Peter:** Though Jesus describes him as the rock on which the church will be built (Matt. 16:16-18), Peter is impetuous and his tongue gets him in trouble, most notably when he denies his Lord three times (John 18). Imagine his feelings as the disciples mourn their Lord's death. Perhaps he is thinking, "The last time I saw him I denied him." Like the other disciples, he too is caught up in hopelessness. Still, he is their leader, despite his denials. As their leader, he races to the tomb but apparently isn't convinced—as John is—that his missing Lord has been resurrected. With the other disciples, he waits, uncertain, behind locked doors. He is probably somewhere between the certainty of Mary and the open doubt of Thomas. Only when he sees the Lord firsthand do his puzzlement and fear give way to joy. He then goes on to fulfill his role as the rock on which the church is founded.

**Thomas:** Thomas proves his loyalty (John 11:16) but also voices his skepticism (John 14:5). When something doesn't add up, he is not shy about announcing what he thinks. So he not only wants to see the risen Jesus, he wants to touch his wounds. Thomas moves quickly from distancing himself from the disciples (John 20:24) and open doubt (John 20:25) to making a confession (John 20:28) that is a high point of Scripture and a model for all of us.

■ **Step 3**
**Who Am I? (10 minutes)**

Ask the group members to think about which character in the story—Mary, Peter, Thomas—best represents them and why. For instance, do they identify with the joy that Mary expressed ("I have seen the Lord!"). Do they sometimes find themselves feeling the skepticism and doubt of Thomas, wanting some evidence that Jesus is for real? Or do they see themselves on the roller coaster of faith that Peter experienced?

Group members need not limit themselves to these characterizations; perhaps they saw other traits with which they identify more closely.

Ask everyone to think about this during a minute of silence. Then invite those who wish to do so to share their thoughts (if your group is large, the sharing time can be within the same small groups used during step 2). Stress a nonjudgmental, honest kind of sharing, and set the tone by describing the person with whom you identify and why.

After everyone has had an opportunity to speak, point out that one of the great lessons from the resurrection is that Jesus didn't wait for Mary, Peter, or Thomas to have it all together before he came to them. He didn't come only to those he judged to be more loyal or faithful. He came to all the disciples, just as they were, doubts and all. You may find it helpful to look at Jesus' inclusive words in John 20:17: the resurrection gives each of us the opportunity to be brothers and sisters of Jesus.

■   **Step 4**
    **Closing (5 minutes)**

If you are using the notecard summaries for each session ("This miracle shows me that Jesus . . . "), you may want to ask group members to look at their responses for session 4, which also dealt with resurrection. What additional insights did they gain from the story of Christ's own resurrection?

Ask everyone to turn to John 20:30-31. Read these key verses in unison. Invite group members to say sentence prayers of thanks and praise for God's gift of life.

Distribute Handout 13 ("Follow-up") and encourage group members to read it at home.

## Options

### 1. Alternate Openings

■  Ask group members to think of something that is possible but so far from probable that they would be completely amazed if it really happened (for instance, that they win a full-ride scholarship to Harvard or that their parents buy them a sports car for graduation or that someone who is critically ill is suddenly healed). It doesn't matter if the event is serious or light. When all have thought of something, invite them to share their ideas with the group to make the transition to today's story. None of the disciples, in their wildest dreams, believed that Jesus could and would be resurrected from the dead.

■  Show a scene from a violent TV show or film where several people are killed. Keep a body count as the scene progresses (for example, the movie *Rambo* has a short scene during which well over fifty people are killed). Talk about what impact seeing so many fake deaths has on us. How do they affect our feelings and fears about death? Do they make us less aware of the grim realities of death and the fantastic nature of the resurrection?

## 2. Alternate Bible Reading

If you'd prefer not to use the Wangerin account of the resurrection, have the group read John 20 as "reader's theater." You will need readers for the lines of Mary, the angels, Jesus, the disciples, Thomas, and a narrator (who reads all lines not in quotation marks).

After the reading, use the "character sketches" activity as described in step 2, or try the "Questions, Questions" option below.

## 3. Questions, Questions

Rather than use the character sketches described in step 2, have each small group come up with three questions to ask of its assigned character (Mary or Peter or Thomas). These should be questions that probe into the character's faith or lack of faith. They should also be questions that group members really would like answered. Have each group jot down their questions on a sheet of newsprint under their character's name. Allow about five minutes for this.

Then quickly appoint a panel to represent Mary, Peter, and Thomas. Let the panel members grapple with the questions from the groups. Use their answers as a basis for further discussion.

Follow this by inviting each person to jot down one question he or she would like to ask God about his or her own faith (this will replace the "Who Am I?" activity of step 3). Share answers as group members are willing to do so.

## 4. Alternate Closing

Invite each person to mention one thing that he or she has found helpful in times of doubt. Close with a guided prayer: you (leader) say the name of a person in your group; everyone then silently prays that God will give that person strength to deal with doubt and will help him or her know the joy of Mary when she said, "I have seen the Lord!"

# 6 THE FIRST AND LAST WORDS

## Scripture

John 21

## Purpose

What do you call it when you fish all night with not a nibble, and then, on the advice of a stranger on the shore, cast your net on the right side of the boat and bring in a haul so large that the sea seems to be boiling with fish? It is a sign—a sign to the disciples that without Jesus they can do nothing. It is a sign that the time has arrived for them to become "fishers of men." The last chapter of John's gospel contains Jesus' final sign and his final words. The instructions given to Peter are for all of us.

This session has three goals:

■ to describe the two miracles in this chapter
■ to explore our need for forgiveness and see that Jesus accepts us when we stumble
■ to respond to the challenges "feed my sheep" and "follow me"

## Perspective

Apparently Peter liked to fish in his underwear. But when the nets are filled with fish and John figures out that the know-it-all on the shore really does know it all, Peter gets so excited that he first gets dressed (you don't greet your Lord half-naked) and then plunges into the sea. His eagerness is understandable—a lot of unfinished business remains between Jesus and Peter. And now, by a charcoal fire on the shores of the Sea of Galilee, this business is settled.

We remember that it was by another charcoal fire, in the courtyard of the high priest, that Peter had denied Jesus three times—this despite an earlier boast that he was willing to follow Jesus even to death (John 13:37). But when the questions got up-close and personal in the courtyard, Peter lied to save his neck.

Now on the beach, by the fire, Jesus asks Peter a question: "Simon, son of John, do you love me?" That's a crucial question. Jesus establishes three times that the one requirement for us serving in his kingdom is not perfection. It's our love for him. However imperfect that love itself may be, that's what Jesus seeks.

Notice that Jesus uses Peter's old name: Simon. It's as if Jesus can't call him Peter (petra, rock) anymore because there in the courtyard Peter had acted more like quicksand than a rock. Then the Lord repeats his question, and repeats it once more, so that the connection to Peter's triple denial is painfully obvious: "Simon, son of John, do you love me?"

In anguish over his sin, Peter blurts out, "Lord, you know all things; you know that I love you." You know, Lord, how I fail you. You know how my good intentions turn into bad results. You know me through and through—the best parts of me and the worst.

Jesus indeed knows everything about Peter, and in a quiet act of grace he chooses to forgive and restore him. There is a place for Peter in Jesus' kingdom. Jesus needs him to be both a fisher of men and a shepherd, but first he must be a disciple. "Follow me" are almost the last words Jesus speaks to Peter in the gospel of John. In Matthew they are the first words Jesus speaks to Peter (Matt. 4:19).

Regardless of whatever else it may be, the call of Jesus is always a call to personal discipleship. Whatever the task and wherever the setting, the first and last words Jesus speaks to Peter and to us are "follow me."

Jesus wants Peter to be a rock, a rock that will become the cornerstone on which the church is built. Life for Peter the apostle will be different than it was for Simon Peter the disciple or Simon the fisherman. Jesus' sheep need to be fed, and to do this Peter has to be obedient and submit to God. In fact, Jesus indicates that Peter certainly will die for Jesus' sake, but doing so will be an act of obedience, not self-glorification.

God looks at us in the same way he looks at Peter. God sees us as we are—a mixture of good and bad, bravery and fear, strength and weakness, light and shadow—and offers us a place in his kingdom. The answer to the question of "now what?" as we finish John's gospel is simply "follow me."

## Materials

1. Handouts 14-17
2. Pens or pencils
3. Bibles
4. Notecards
5. Newsprint/markers
6. Videotape of *Rocky* or great sports finishes
7. VCR and monitor
8. "What If I Stumble?" recording by d.c. Talk (optional)

## Procedure

■ **Step 1**
**Fantastic Finishes (10-15 minutes)**
Begin the session by showing a video clip of a dramatic, come-from-behind finish. For example, show the last few minutes of the fight in *Rocky*, or some sports video clips like the 1951 "Shot Heard Round the World" New York Giants baseball playoff win

(where the announcer screams "The Giants Win the Pennant!" over and over), the 1988 World Series where an injured Kirk Gibson comes off the bench to hit a game-winning home run, or other memorable moments. Video rental stores abound with these "greatest sports moments" collections. Or get creative and put together your own cliché-filled narration about "against all odds, come from behind, they said he couldn't do it, snatching victory from the jaws of defeat, the thrill of victory and the agony of defeat, staring defeat in the face and refusing to give in, etc."

You'll want to make this an upbeat, fun way to start this session. After the video, ask group members to tell about a time they failed at something, got a second (or third or fourth) chance, and eventually succeeded.

After everyone has had a chance to share, you may want to ask the group if they know the song "What If I Stumble?" by d.c. Talk. The writer wonders "if the love will continue" when he "loses his step" and when his walk "becomes a crawl." He wonders what will happen if he stumbles and falls. If you can get a copy of the recording, play it for your group.

It's not clear if "will the love continue?" refers to God's love continuing or to the love of a Christian artist's fans continuing if the singer did stumble in his faith. You can use this ambiguity to point out that our failures can affect both our relationship with God and with other people. That's one reason why Jesus publicly restores Peter after his denial. For Peter to have the respect of the other disciples, they have to see that Jesus forgives, accepts, and loves Peter.

Before focusing on that encounter, move on to step 2, which is meant to help heighten our awareness of our need to confess.

■ **Step 2**
**Any Alligators in Your Lake? (10 minutes)**
Distribute Handout 14 ("Any Alligators in Your Lake?"), which tells the story of an unfortunate encounter between an alligator and a woman who chose to ignore the threat the gator presented. Ask for a volunteer to read the brief story to the group.

After reading the story, ask the group to identify some "alligators" that may be lurking around in people's lives today: threats from within or without that we may choose to ignore but that can badly hurt us. Keep the discussion general at this point. Use a sheet of newsprint to jot down ideas that the group mentions. Below are several examples:

- an addiction to drugs, smoking, alcohol, pornography, sex
- an unconfessed sin
- strained relationship with parents
- AIDS or other diseases
- cheating, lying, phoniness, dishonesty
- having racist attitudes and actions
- using friendships for our own gain
- valuing possessions more than relationships

Point out how in very dramatic situations, such as a family member with an addiction problem, or in less dramatic situations, such as when a friend lets another friend down, we cannot move forward until we confess what the problem is. To deal with the situation we have to admit it exists. If we cannot do that we are in danger of being devoured by what we choose to ignore. That is why God wants us to confess our sins to him. Confession is the path to wholeness and health.

Explain that John's gospel ends with Jesus gently helping Peter face the problem of his denial of Jesus. Peter was running away from the problem by attempting to return to his old life of fishing. But then Jesus intervenes in a miraculous way.

## ■ Step 3
### A Lakeside Encounter (15-20 minutes)

Read John 21 with the group. This chapter features a lot of dialogue, much of it between Peter and Jesus, so you may want to try the familiar "reader's theater" approach. You'll need people to read the lines of Peter, the disciples, Jesus, and John. A narrator can read all the lines not in quotation marks.

If you prefer, simply take turns reading the chapter aloud. Or have group members read the chapter quietly to themselves.

Should your group not be familiar with the story of Peter's denial (John 18:15-18, 25-27), take time to read it now before using the handout.

Distribute Handout 15 ("A Lakeside Encounter") and give group members five minutes to complete the ten multiple-choice questions under the heading "The Story" (they can do this in pairs, if they wish). They should save the two "My Story" questions for personal completion later.

Discuss the responses to the multiple-choice questions with the entire group. Note that several of the questions give people a chance to add other responses of their own. Keep in mind, too, that multiple responses are appropriate in many cases. Discussion, not "right answers," is the goal.

Guidelines follow each question below.

1. What does the fact that the disciples go fishing tell you?

   a. They want to have some fun.
   b. They are broke and need to catch and sell some fish.
   c. They have decided to go back to their pre-Jesus life.
   d. They love fishing more than they love Jesus.
   e. Other?_____

An all-night excursion using fishing nets sounds more like commercial fishing than recreation. Perhaps Peter and the others have indeed decided to go back to their pre-Jesus life. It's almost as if they don't know what else to do at this point. They've seen the risen Lord twice but are uncertain what he wants them to do next. So they return to something familiar and comfortable.

2. After fishing all night, the disciples catch nothing. Then, on advice from a stranger, they catch so many they can't haul in their net. If I had been fishing with them, I would have thought—

   a. "I wonder who that guy is who gave us such good advice?"
   b. "I guess our luck took a turn for the better."
   c. "This is unbelievable! Fantastic! How can it be?"
   d. "Only Jesus could work a miracle like this."
   e. "Can't wait to sell all these fish!"
   f. Other? _____

Note that the question calls for a personal response and therefore has no "right" answers. After the excitement of hauling in a net so full of fish that normally it would have ripped the net apart (response *c*), attention would naturally focus on the one who worked the miracle (responses *a* and *d*). Perhaps all of the disciples immediately suspect that it was none other than their risen Lord, but only John says so directly.

3. When John says, "It is the Lord," Peter jumps in and starts swimming for shore. Why?

   a. He knows the boat will sink when all those fish are hauled in.
   b. He can't wait to see Jesus—they have lots to talk about.
   c. He wants to show Jesus he's still the leader of the disciples.
   d. He's just happy to see Jesus.
   e. Other?_____

No doubt Peter is overjoyed at seeing Jesus on the shore, and, being impulsive, he quickly dresses and leaps into the waves. But there's something else behind his joy: he and Jesus have unfinished business (response *b*). Peter has yet to resolve a major, major rift between him and his Lord. Perhaps this has been eating away at his conscience, and now he sees a chance to set things right with the Master.

4. The disciples do not dare ask the man on the beach who he is. Why not?

   a. They're not sure it's the Lord.
   b. They're in awe of him.
   c. They don't want to embarrass themselves.
   d. They're afraid of being reprimanded for asking.
   e. Other?_____

Why does John bother to tell us that none of the disciples dare to ask Jesus who he is, though they know it is truly the Lord? It's a touching, wonderfully human detail, probably stemming from the absolute awe that's inspired not only by the miracle itself but by simply being in the presence of the risen Lord (response *b*). There may also be an element of not wanting to embarrass themselves—if they ask Jesus who he is, he could think they really didn't know the man with whom they've spent three years. And that could be embarrassing (response *c*). Jesus would be unlikely to reprimand them for asking, given his gentle response to Mary's uncertainty in the garden by the tomb.

5. John reports Jesus' miracles as signs that have several meanings. Of what might the great catch of fish be a sign? (John 5:15 may provide a clue.)

   a. Without Jesus, we can't do anything; with him, all things are possible.
   b. Jesus changes our luck from bad to good.
   c. Always listen to Jesus.
   d. It's time for the disciples to get on with their mission: becoming fishers of men.
   e. Other?_____

Jesus says in John 15:5 that if we abide in him, we will bear much fruit, but apart from him we can do nothing. The miracle in John 21 is a sign of the truth of these words (response *a*). Life without Jesus is as empty as their fishing nets. But with Jesus there is a fantastic catch. It is time for the disciples to get on with their mission—not as fishermen but as fishers of men (response *c*).

6. Why does Jesus ask Peter "Do you love me?" not once but three times?

   a. To make sure Peter (and the other disciples) get the connection to the three times Peter denied Jesus.
   b. To make Peter squirm a little.
   c. To show Peter (and the other disciples) that Peter was completely forgiven and restored.
   d. To emphasize that the most important question anyone can be asked is "Do you love Jesus?"
   e. Other?_____

Response *c* gets at the heart of the matter. It's important that this restoration be public, in full view of the other disciples who are present, so that Peter can resume his leadership position among the disciples and get on with the work Jesus has called him to do.

7. I imagine Peter answering Jesus—

   a. Loudly, confidently, boldly
   b. Softly, humbly, urgently
   c. Reluctantly, as if angry or upset
   d. Other?_____

When you've truly messed up and are then given a second chance, there's no room for anything else but humility (response *b*). True, by the time Peter answers the same question the third time, his feelings are hurt and the humility is laced with an anguished kind of urgency: "Lord, you know all things. You know that I love you."

8. What shows that Jesus hasn't given up on Peter?

    a. He asks Peter, "Do you love me?"
    b. He gives Peter something important to do ("feed my sheep").
    c. He restores Peter in front of the other disciples.
    d. He tells Peter to follow him.
    e. Other?_____

This is intended to be one of those "all of the above" responses. See what your group thinks and why. Clearly, Jesus hasn't given up on Peter; he has something of extreme importance for him to do. This second chance must bring hope to Peter. He needs to be reconciled to Jesus so that the work of the kingdom can go forward.

9. "Feed my sheep" means—

    a. Become a shepherd—it pays better than fishing.
    b. Give people food when they're hungry.
    c. Tell people the good news about Jesus.
    d. Help people grow in their relationship to God.
    e. Other?_____

"Feed my sheep" is something of an abbreviated great commission (responses *c* and *d*). It implies that Peter must "make disciples of all nations, baptizing them . . . and teaching them to obey everything I have commanded you" (Matt. 28:19-20).

This commissioning to be a shepherd means that Peter does indeed need to be prepared to lay down his life for Jesus' sake, just as he once said he was willing to do. That is what a good shepherd does for his flock. Tell your group that, according to tradition, Peter did indeed die for Jesus' sake—he was crucified upside down.

10. After this encounter, Peter probably felt—

    a. Worried that he might be crucified like Jesus.
    b. Relieved that Jesus wasn't angry with him.
    c. Humbly grateful for being forgiven, restored.
    d. Proud of the important work he had been given to do.
    e. Ready to do his job as leader of the disciples.
    f. Other?_____

The Bible does not spell out how Peter felt after this encounter. There is, however, an interesting exchange between Jesus and Peter concerning what may or may not happen to John. Perhaps Peter wonders if John, too, will die for the cause. But Jesus, in effect, tells him to mind his own business, which is following the Lord and doing his work. Having been forgiven and restored, Peter is now ready to do exactly that.

■ **Step 4**
   **My Story**

At the end of Handout 15 are a couple of questions that attempt to apply today's passage on a more personal level ("My Story"). Give the group time to think about each question and to jot a brief response. Be sensitive—don't push for answers, but don't move so quickly that the young people in your group won't have a chance to respond.

■ If Jesus looked at your life this week, would he need to ask: "Do you love me?"

This is the type of question that you (the leader) may want to answer first. Be vulnerable, and create a spirit of openness. This may also be a good time to personalize the illustrations from the alligator story earlier in the session. Perhaps the reason that someone may feel unable to show love for Jesus is an issue that needs to be confessed and dealt with.

■ As the gospel of John closes, Jesus gives clear directions to Peter ("feed my sheep" and "follow me"). What direction might Jesus be giving you as our study of John ends?

You may wish to write "feed my sheep" and "follow me" on a couple of sheets of newsprint. Then record the group's responses as they discuss how we can obey these commands in our daily living.

By way of summary, point out that being a disciple starts with being devoted to Christ. Too often we get caught up in what we can *do* for Jesus, when he really wants us to *be* disciples. Our "doing" then flows out of our "being." Peter boasted about what he was going to do for Christ, but his boasting was based on his own strength. If we rely on our own resources, eventually we will burn out.

In *My Utmost for His Highest,* Oswald Chambers says it this way: "If I am devoted solely to the cause of humanity, I will soon be exhausted and come to the point where my love will waver and stumble. But if I love Jesus Christ personally and passionately, I can serve humanity, even though people may treat me like a 'doormat.' The secret of a disciple's life is devotion to Jesus Christ."

■ **Step 5**
   **Closing (5-10 minutes)**

If you are using the notecard summaries for each session ("This story shows me that Jesus . . . "), have group members take a moment to complete a notecard for today's session. See Option 4 ("Review") for a suggestion on how to use the cards for a quick review of this course.

In a recent research project for CRC Publications, high school youth leaders indicated that the most important biblical theme to their kids was forgiveness (followed by grace and love/joy). You will want to close today's session and this study with a strong affirmation that when we stumble and fall, God's love will indeed continue for us as it did for Peter and help us get up and move ahead.

Say something like the above to your group. Then ask the group to turn to 1 John 1:8-9 in their Bibles. Read this passage in unison.

For your closing prayer, give group members a moment of silence in which they may bring to God personal matters for which they need forgiveness. End the quiet time by expressing thanks to God for giving all of us "a second chance" by forgiving us and restoring us to himself.

Before group members leave, invite them to complete the evaluation form (Handout 17). A leader's evaluation is found at the end of this leader's guide. We thank you for taking time to complete the forms and mail them in.

Distribute Handout 16 ("Follow-up") for group members who are using it to guide their at-home devotions.

## Options

### 1. Alternate Opening

If getting a video isn't going to work for you, begin the session by telling a story of a "most embarrassing moment" for you personally, a time when you did something really dumb, or a time when you failed miserably at something. Then ask group members to recall similar instances from their own experience. Commend those who share a story—being able to laugh at ourselves, or being able to tell about a personal failure, are marks of maturity.

### 2. Alternate Closing

Handout 16 ("Follow-up") explains how to put together an ACTS prayer (ACTS is an acronym for adoration, confession, thanksgiving, and supplication). Distribute Handout 16 and quickly skim the explanation of ACTS. Then lead a time of guided prayer, giving group members an opportunity to offer sentence prayers of adoration, confession (these can be silent), thanksgiving, and supplication.

### 3. Alternate Story Discussion

If you'd rather not use the multiple-choice questions to discuss today's story (step 3), divide into small groups and have each group write its own questions on a sheet of newsprint. Assign part of John 21 to each group, as follows:

■ John 21:1-14
■ John 21:13-19
■ John 21:20-25

Encourage the groups to ask at least two questions about the meaning of the story and two questions that attempt to apply the story to our daily lives.

Have the small groups lead a discussion of their questions with the rest of the class.

## 4. Review

If you have extra time and if your group has been using notecards each week to record their responses to "This miracle shows me that Jesus . . . ," you may want to use the cards for a quick review. Have group members recall one of the miracles we studied, then sample several notecard responses to that miracle. Review all six miracles in this way.

*Six Unsolved Mysteries*

# LEADER EVALUATION FORM

## Background

Size of group:

☐ under 5
☐ 5-9
☐ 10-15
☐ more than 15

School grade of participants:

☐ grade 10
☐ grade 11
☐ grade 12
☐ post-high

Length of group sessions:

☐ under 30 minutes
☐ 30-45 minutes
☐ 45-60 minutes
☐ over 60 minutes

Please check items that describe you:

☐ male
☐ female
☐ ordained or professional church
   staff layperson
☐ elder or deacon
☐ professional teacher
☐ church school or catechism teacher
   (three or more years)
☐ volunteer youth leader

## Handouts for Group Members

In general, I—

☐ did not use the handouts
☐ used the handouts frequently

Please check items that describe
the handouts:

☐ too few
☐ too many
☐ helpful
☐ not helpful

The "Follow-up" suggestions for at-home
activities were

☐ not distributed
☐ generally ignored by group members
☐ used by a few group members
☐ used by most group members

## Leader's Guide and Group Process

Please check items that describe the
activities suggested for each group
session:

☐ varied
☐ monotonous
☐ creative
☐ dull
☐ clear
☐ unclear
☐ interesting to participants
☐ uninteresting to participants
☐ too many
☐ too few

Please check the items that describe the Perspective material provided in the leader's guide:

☐ helpful, stimulating
☐ not helpful or stimulating
☐ overly complex, long
☐ about right level of difficulty
☐ clear
☐ unclear

Please check those procedures that worked best for you:

☐ small group discussion
☐ whole group discussion
☐ individuals working by themselves
☐ handouts
☐ reader's theater for Bible passages
☐ writing assignments
☐ use of Options
☐ supplementing with my own activities
☐ other _____

The course in general was true to the Reformed/Presbyterian tradition.

☐ agree
☐ disagree
☐ not sure

Please check the items that describe the group sessions:

☐ lively
☐ dull
☐ dominated by leader
☐ involved most participants
☐ relevant to lives of participants
☐ irrelevant to lives of participants
☐ worthwhile
☐ not worthwhile

In general, I would rate this material as—

☐ excellent
☐ good
☐ fair
☐ poor

Additional comments on any aspect of this program:

Name (optional): _____

Church: _____

City/State/Province: _____

Please send comments to

CRC Publications
Prime-Time Bible Studies
2850 Kalamazoo Ave. SE
Grand Rapids, MI 49560

Thank you!